East Anglia
PANORAMAS

STUNNING PHOTOGRAPHS OF EASTERN ENGLAND

JOHN POTTER

MYRIAD BOOKS LONDON

CONTENTS

NORFOLK & LINCOLNSHIRE   4

SUFFOLK & CAMBRIDGESHIRE   56

BEDFORDSHIRE, HERTFORDSHIRE & ESSEX   74

NORFOLK & LINCOLNSHIRE

The area around the Wash and the north Norfolk coast is one of the most beautiful coastlines in the whole of Britain. Much of it has been designated as an area of outstanding natural beauty, famous for its wide sandy beaches, pine forests, saltmarsh, pretty villages and seaside resorts

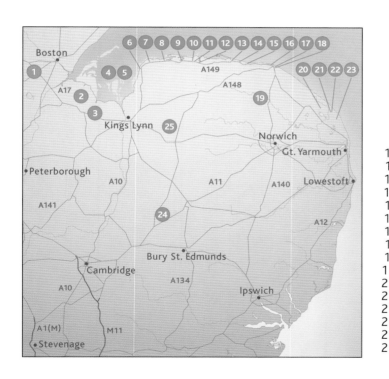

1	SWINESHEAD DAFFODILS	6
2	GEDNEY MARSH WIND FARM	8
3	SUTTON BRIDGE PATROL BOATS	10
4	HEACHAM	12
5	LAVENDER AT HEACHAM	14
6	HUNSTANTON	16
7	HOLME NEXT THE SEA	18
8	BRANCASTER	20
9	BURNHAM OVERY STAITHE	22
10	HOLKHAM BEACH	24
11	HOLKHAM HALL	26
12	WELLS-NEXT-THE-SEA	28
13	CLEY MILL	30
14	SALTHOUSE	32
15	WEYBOURNE	34
16	EAST RUNTON	36
17	CROMER PIER	38
18	CROMER BEACH	40
19	BLICKLING HALL	42
20	HICKLING BROAD	44
21	HORSEY MILL	46
22	HORSEY SEAL COLONY	48
23	EAST SOMERTON	50
24	HOW HILL	52
25	CASTLE ACRE	54

OPPOSITE – CROMER

A view towards the magnificent East Cliffs at Cromer – the beautiful Norfolk seaside resort made popular by the Victorians

SWINESHEAD DAFFODILS

Kite-surfers at Hunstanton revel in ideal conditions as strong north-easterly winds sweep in off the North Sea. Kite-surfing is the fastest growing watersport in the world and some of the best surf and wind in the UK is to be found on the east coast of Norfolk. Hunstanton, or 'Sunny Hunny', is best known for its famous striped cliffs which look like a giant piece of red and white coconut ice. The cliffs also provide fossil-collectors with a fabulous supply of specimens.

HOLME NEXT THE SEA

Holme next the Sea is an unspoilt village where the Peddars Way, a long-distance path that follows the route of a Roman road, comes to its seaward end. The village and its surrounding area is designated as an area of outstanding natural beauty, and the Norfolk Coastal Path that follows the coast from Cromer can be easily accessed, providing a wide range of opportunities for walking. The beaches here are blissfully quiet and backed by marram grass-covered sand dunes, seen here rippling in the breeze.

BRANCASTER

The North Norfolk area of outstanding natural beauty is a haven for wildlife and migratory birds, and the ideal place for beachcombing, birdwatching and sailing. Flagstaff House, situated next to the Staithe, was once the home of Captain Woodget of *The Cutty Sark*. This view of the sandy creek, a salt water inlet running out to the sea at low tide, illustrates what an ideal spot this is for sailing. Crabbing is a very popular pastime, particularly when the tide is falling and crab lines can be purchased from the boathouse. Apparently bacon is the best bait to use!

HOLKHAM BEACH

The stretch of coastline from Holkham to Wells consists of salt marshes which were gradually reclaimed from the sea between 1639 and 1859. These sand dunes are formed on old shingle ridges, and the topography is constantly changing in this sometimes harsh but dramatically beautiful area. The National Nature Reserve at Holkham is a stunning location where a diverse mixture of wildlife and habitats come together. The dunes are home to many wildflowers including marsh helleborine, southern marsh-orchid and corn salad.

HOLKHAM HALL

Holkham Hall is pictured here in its magnificent grounds at first light. Holkham Park is open to the public throughout the year except Christmas Day. There are many tracks and paths making access easy for visitors; the woods are home to a large herd of fallow deer and a variety of birdlife. The lake, more than a mile long, was built in 1727 and is fed by seven fresh water springs. During the visitors' season boat trips are available in the electric launch.

WELLS-NEXT-THE-SEA

Cromer is often referred to as 'The Gem of the Norfolk Coast'. This isolated fishing village was 'discovered' in the 18th century by merchants and travellers but it developed slowly due to its remote location. The arrival of the railway in 1877 fuelled its development and by the 1890s it was a thriving holiday resort. Cromer is famous for its elegant pier and theatre, its renowned crabs and its lifeboat – in 1917 coxwain Henry Blogg was awarded the RNLI Gold Medal for services to the Swedish steamship *Fernebo*.

CROMER BEACH

Fringed by the cliffs of north Norfolk, the beautiful sand and shingle beach at Cromer attracts vissitors for its clean sea-bathing and fishing. Together with beach huts (for which there is a waiting list) there are showers for bathers, and the beach is patrolled by lifeguards from May to September. The beach is increasingly popular with surfers, particularly the area near the pier where waves form.

BLICKLING HALL

Constructed between 1616 and 1628 for Sir Henry Hobart, Blickling Hall is a magnificent Jacobean mansion set in beautiful parkland and gardens. Owned by the National Trust, it is situated 1.5 miles north-west of Aylsham on the B1354. There is plenty here for visitors – an exhibition in the Harness Room highlights Blickling's Second World War connections with nearby RAF Oulton and there are country walks within the park plus a lively programme of events, including open-air concerts and theatre.

HICKLING BROAD

The National Nature Reserve at Hickling Broad is the largest in the Norfolk Broads. It covers approximately 1,200 acres, including water's edge reeds and marshlands, which are host to endangered species such as the marsh harrier, swallow tail butterfly and bittern. A regular visitor in the summer is the spoonbill. The Broad is part of the river Thurne system and a magnet for sailors and birdwatchers. The Thurne region, a maze of dykes, rivers and broads, is host to rare wildlife, pretty waterside towns and a variety of windmills.

HORSEY MILL

Horsey Mill is a fully restored drainage windpump which was entirely rebuilt in 1912. Owned by the National Trust since 1948, it has five storeys and provides superb views of the Broads and coast. The mill was restored in 1961 by the Norfolk Windmills Trust but had its fantail blown off, not for the first time, in the October 1987 hurricane. Mills have had many uses over the years, including signalling and storing smuggled contraband.

HORSEY SEAL COLONY

The beach between Horsey and Winterton has provided a safe haven for grey seal (*Halichoerus grypus*) colonies for around two decades. Now numbering approximately 100, the colony returns each year between November and January to give birth to pups. Local people and English Nature's volunteer wardens help to keep an eye on the colony as increasing numbers of visitors are attracted by this wonderful spectacle. Half of the world's population of grey seals are to be found on and around British coasts and the numbers have doubled since 1960.

EAST SOMERTON

Southwold, a unique Suffolk seaside town is a wonderful destination for thousands of holidaymakers each year. Bounded by the North Sea to the east, the river Blyth and Southwold harbour to the south-west, and Buss Creek to the north, the town is almost an island. There are 300 characterful and historic beach huts along the shoreline at Southwold, which evolved from fishermen's and bathing huts. They now change hands for vast sums of money and there is always a waiting list.

WALBERSWICK

From the 13th century to the First World War, Walberswick was a thriving port, trading in bacon, cheese, timber and fish. Now it is a busy and popular tourist resort during the summer, and many of the properties are holiday homes. It is believed that the name Walberswick is derived from the Saxon *Walbert* or *Walhbert*, possibly a landowner, and *wyc* meaning shelter or harbour. The town is famous for hosting the British Open Crabbing Championships each year.

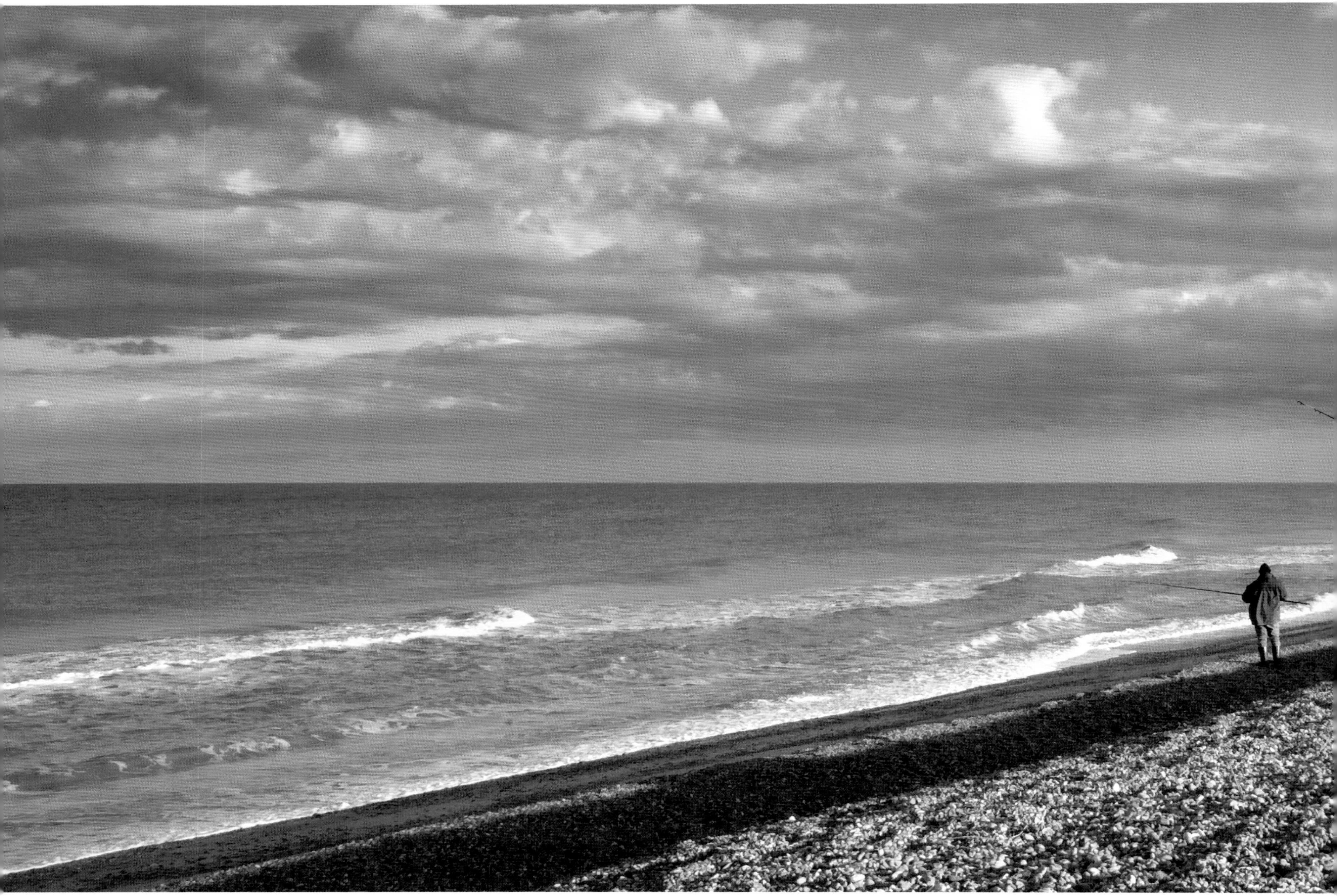

Dunwich was a thriving port in the 12th and 13th centuries, famous the world over for its mariners and shipwrights. The village is steeped in history, and is surrounded by rare and wonderful habitats, including Dunwich Heath, together with large areas of woodland between Dunwich and Walberswick. In the middle ages Dunwich had a sizeable population of around 4,000 inhabitants but centuries of ravaging storms have taken their toll and most of the settlement has been claimed by the sea. Legend has it that at low tide church bells can be heard ringing from the depths of the sea.

FRAMLINGHAM CASTLE

Situated 18 miles north-east of Ipswich, Framlingham Castle is an impressive landmark on the skyline. It has 13 towers linked by a curtain wall. Magnificent views can be enjoyed from the battlements of the town, the reed-fringed mere and surrounding countryside. The castle has quite a chequered history, and over the years has been used as a fortress, an Elizabethan prison, a school and poorhouse. It was here in 1553 that Mary Tudor was proclaimed Queen of England.

SIZEWELL

The nuclear power station at Sizewell dominates this stretch of the Suffolk coast. For 10 years it has supplied almost three per cent of Britain's electricity needs. Construction started in 1988 and in 1995 the station came on-stream. The colours of the power station were carefully selected by the Commission of Fine Arts to blend in with the environment. This coastline is well-known for its gales — when this photograph was taken it was necessary to suspend a large boulder from the tripod to keep the camera still.

ST NEOTS

The gardens of Clare College are sited on ancient fenland bounded on three sides by dykes, and on the fourth side by the river Cam. The gardens form part of the famous Backs — the rear part of many of the colleges which border the river. The gardens at Clare, the second oldest of the Cambridge colleges, were redesigned after the Second World War. A gnarled Judas tree (*Ceris siliquastrum*), a swamp Cypress (*Taxodium distichum*), chestnuts and old yew trees all add to the unique atmosphere and character of this beautiful garden set in the heart of the city.

CLARE

The riverside village of Pavenham is situated six miles north-west of Bedford on a loop of the the river Ouse. The village is surrounded by gentle rolling hills and rich farmland and there are some delightful footpaths inviting visitors to explore this pretty village. One path leads down to the Ouse which meanders its way lazily through a wooded valley with water meadows. In the past, reeds from the riverbank were used for the making of mats and Pavenham mats were once used on the floors of the Palace of Westminster.

SANDY LODGE

A picture postcard village stuated between Sible Hedingham and Thaxted, Finchingfield is renowned as the most photographed village in Essex. It is filled with painted medieval houses, known as 'Cabbaches'. The building which houses the Causeway Tea Cottage dates from 1490. The village has a picturesque pond and village green, a windmill and the beautiful church of St John the Baptist with its eye-catching Norman tower. The name Finchingfield is derived from Saxon times, when Finc's folk made a clearing in the forest for a new settlement.

90

This handsome tower mill was built in 1804 by John Webb, a local landowner, farmer and innkeeper using bricks and tiles from his own quarry in the Chelmer valley. At this time the population of London was rapidly expanding and the mill supplied the city with flour. The walls measure 4ft at the base and are 18 inches thick just below the cap. Towards the end of the 19th century the mill became uneconomic and in 1904 it was closed down and its sails locked up. It was restored in 1970 and is now an agricultural museum.

94

FLATFORD MILL

Flatford Mill lies at the heart of Constable Country in the Vale of Dedham on the river Stour. Many of the buildings feature in the idyllic pastoral paintings of John Constable, the famous landscape painter who was brought up close by in East Bergholt. His family owned Flatford Mill and, as a boy, he spent a great deal of time there learning the miller's trade. His most famous painting, *The Hay Wain*, captures the scene across the mill pond and includes Willie Lott's cottage (seen here), the home of one of the mill-hands at Flatford.

BRIGHTLINGSEA

Situated between Colchester and Clacton, where the river Colne flows into the sea, Brightlingsea is the only Cinque Port in Essex. In the centre of the town is the 600-year-old Jacob's Hall, one of the oldest timber-framed buildings in England. The waterfront boasts colourful beach huts, a lively sailing scene and an attractive small beach which looks across to Mersea Island. At the Aldous Heritage Dock many historic fishing smacks can be seen; the town has a thiving preservation society which cares for these attractive boats and organises regular races on the Colne – a tradition which dates back to the late 18th century.

First published in 2007 by Myriad Books Limited, 35 Bishopsthorpe Road, London SE26 4PA

Photographs and text copyright © John Potter

John Potter has asserted his right under the Copyright, Designs and Patents Act 1998 to be identified as the author of this work.

ISBN 1 84746 022 4   EAN 978 1 84746 022 6   Designed by Phillip Appleton   Printed in China   www.myriadbooks.com